LEGACY COALITION PRESENTS

Grandparenting Matters

LARRY FOWLER

Founder, Legacy Coalition

This book belongs to:

_____

Legacy
COALITION

LegacyCoalition.com

Legacy
COALITION

Unless otherwise noted, Scripture quotations are taken from
the New International Version copyright 2011 by Zondervan
Corporation.

Table of Contents
AN OVERVIEW OF THE SEMINAR

About Legacy Coalition

WE GRANDPARENT ON PURPOSE
So our grandchildren's grandchildren follow Christ

We Create That Impact By...

Awakening Grandparents
to their full influence potential

Re-Igniting Passion
in grandparents for their grandchildren

Redefining Grandparenting
to align with Scripture

Strengthening Relationships
between grandparents and parents

- We convene the top Christian thought leaders on grandparenting at the only global conference on grandparenting.
- We make unlearning and learning accessible through in-person, virtual, and digital seminars, podcasts, social media blogs, and other online programming.
- We encourage churches to launch grandparenting ministries through the activities of our ambassadors.
- We create practical tools and resources and provide solutions through those resources, conversations, and networking.

Here's What We Do

Share
the vision for grandparenting in a way that impassions and resonates

Help
grandparents unlearn cultural definitions of grandparenting & learn God's purpose in grandparenting

Disrupt
the current church understanding of grandparenting

Provide
practical solutions for overcoming obstacles

Join Us

Learn more about us at:

legacycoalition.com

Share your thoughts at:

info@legacycoalition.com

Follow us on social media

Declare that you
are an intentional
Christian grandparent!

About the Founder

Larry Fowler is the founder of Legacy Coalition. His vision for a national grandparenting ministry brought together a gifted team of family, children's, and youth ministry leaders to launch this movement of God.

His more than forty years of ministry includes experience as a youth pastor, and as part of the Awana staff, a missionary, trainer, international director, and executive leader.

Larry has authored five books on children's and family ministry and was recognized for his lifetime of contribution to children's ministry by the International Network of Children's Ministry with their national Legacy Award.

Larry and his wife, Diane, live in Riverside, CA. They have two children and seven grandchildren.

Introduction

Grandparenting is an adventure that takes some by surprise. Others enter grandparenting after a long season of anticipation. But nearly all of us embark on this wonderful journey with pure joy! Though many grandparents accept this new season with excitement, most have never thought about their Biblical role and responsibility in this cherished but sometimes challenging season.

Larry Fowler, founder of Legacy Coalition, began to write and teach this seminar all over the United States in 2017 and 2018. His teaching impacted thousands of grandparents as he spoke wise words of encouragement, inspiration, challenge, and hope.

As demand for the seminar grew, it became clear that the Legacy Coalition needed to make this Biblical instruction more widely available, so we now offer the seminar through a "live" webinar and in a digital format to be used in small groups.

The seminar helps you overcome grandparenting obstacles, equips you with best practices to implement in passing on your faith, and provides a strategy for reaching the hearts of your grandchildren.

Our desire is for you to be awakened to the role no one else in your family can fill. God designed you to be a spiritual influencer to multiple generations. We thank you for taking this God-given role seriously by embarking on this life-changing series with us.

May the Lord bless you and keep you until you reach the finish line.

Brenda Peitzman

Director of Resource Development
Legacy Coalition

Participant Expectations

This seminar was designed to encourage and equip Christian grandparents by teaching Biblical principles that will inspire you to leave a legacy of faith to your grandchildren. You'll enjoy 14-30 minute sessions of teaching that include practical demonstrations to help Godly principles stick with you. Discussion breaks enable you to share with and to learn from other grandparents.

It is important for you to have your own workbook, as there are illustrations, blanks to fill in, and areas for personal reflection. We trust this workbook will become a valuable resource for you as you learn how to pass on a Godly legacy to your grandchildren.

Additional helpful resources for grandparents may be found at: **legacycoalition.com/store**

Session Running Times

Session 1
Part A......................15:24
Part B......................24:47

Session 2
Part A......................28:54
Part B......................13:48

Session 3
Part A......................13:42
Part B......................24:54

Session 4
Part A......................29:24
Part B......................21:33

Session 5
Part A......................19:02
Part B......................14:46
Part C......................17:53

Session 6......................20:24

Leader Instructions

This 6-session study is divided into 12 segments, with a set of ques¬ tions at the end of each segment. You can make this a 6-week study, or extend it up to 12 weeks if your schedule permits, to allow more time for group discussions.

Preview the segment(s) before each meeting with your group to famil- iarize yourself with the content and questions. The optimal discussion group size is typically 8-10 people. If you are meeting in a large room, you may want to use round tables to facilitate transparent conversations.

Emphasize the importance of confidentiality within the groups; make it a safe place for participants to care for one another as they share trials they are facing. Pray for one another and each other's families throughout the study, using Scripture as your basis for direction

or advice. This is not a place for counseling, but for encouragement, support, and help in implementing this teaching from God's Word.

As the leader, you may want to order books or other resources to share with the group as you learn together how to be more intentional in your role as a Biblical grandparent. Additional resources are available at: legacycoalition.com/store.

Before you begin watching Session 1A, consider having your participants get acquainted by discussing the fol¬ lowing within their group(s).

Share with the others how many grandkids you have, their ages and where they live.

Describe how grandparenting has been different than parenting for you.

The Amazing Influence of a Grandparent

The Amazing Influence of a Grandparent

Two Phrases to Remember

1. Intentional Christian Grandparenting

2. Grandparenting Matters!

> *We are praying for God to raise up a national movement of intentional Christian grandparents!*

Larry Fowler | Founder, Legacy Coalition

What did you learn about grandparenting from your grandparents?

 Discuss

1. What kind of examples did you have?
   a) I never knew my grandparents.
   b) I knew them, but they had no spiritual influence in my life.
   c) I had Godly grandparents who deeply impacted my life.
   d) I had a mixed bag.

2. How does this impact the way you desire to grandparent?

3. Which grandparent in your life had the greatest influence on you?

The Amazing Influence of a Grandparent

Five Reasons to Focus on Grandparenting

1. **Scripture Says:** Involvement by grandparents in a child's spiritual development is Biblical.

"...Teach your children _____ your children's children."
DEUTERONOMY 4:9

To teach is to repeatedly instruct. This is more than just an idea or a thought. It is a COMMAND from God!

2. **Incredible Potential:** Grandparents are _____ only to parents in their potential to influence children spiritually.

You will be with them all through childhood, while teachers or coaches or youth workers are only for a year or a season.

You have a valued relationship with your grandchildren that is nurtured from the moment they are born. There is unconditional love that others do not have for them.

> *We must understand the biblical purpose of a grandparent. This is God's idea — that you would partner with God so the next generation would know and love Jesus.*
>
> Dr Josh Mulvihill | Author, Biblical Grandparenting

There are currently more grandparents who are
Gen-Xers than there are grandparents who are Boomers.

In the United States:
There are 30 million Christian grandparents.

- The average age of becoming a grandparent is _____ .

- The average age of all grandparents is _____ .

- The average number of grandchildren is _____ .

These numbers translate into approximately 100 million
grandchildren to impact!

3. Eager Audience: Grandparents are eager to be spiritual influencers of
their grandchildren; in fact, they are often _____
than the parents.

*Our GRAND vision is that 30 million
grandparents would become spiritual
influencers of their grandchildren.*

Larry Fowler | Founder, Legacy Coalition

Statistics show that kids who are taken to church by their grandparents are more likely to attend regularly.

4. The Cultural Deceit:
   A "_____" mentality downplays and inhibits family ties.

   Culture tells us that it's time to retire and go play, travel, and rest. The lure of leisure is promoted in our culture. This is retirement narcissism—"What is best for me?" Society emboldens our self-centered lifestyle.

   Grandparents' worth is as a playmate.

5. We Can Do Better: "_____ out of _____ Christian grandparents believe something other than discipleship of grandchildren is more important. For a high percentage of Christian grandparents, the priority was encouragement, support, or friendship. For the majority of grandparents, these approaches were the end goal rather than a means to intentionally help grandchildren grow spiritually. Numerous grandparents in these 3 categories spoke about the importance of the spiritual growth of grandchildren. However, it was not reflected in how they operated as a grandparent, revealing the spiritual life of a grandchild was not as important as they claimed." – Dr. Josh Mulvihill

   The message of culture that says the priority of grandparents is encouragement, support, and friendship, needs to be challenged.

   According to Dr. Mulvihill, many Christian grandparents have a pray and play mentality. They become a trusted companion, spoiler, playmate, and friend. But they do not have a perspective of being a significant spiritual influencer in the life of their grandchild.*

*Content from Biblical Grandparenting by Dr. Josh Mulvihill

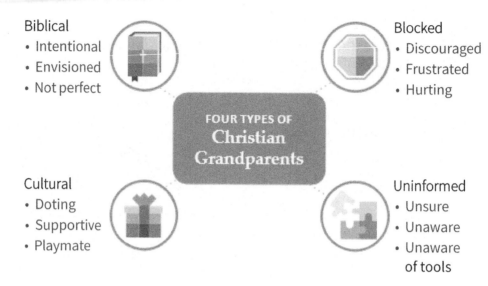

Biblical
- Intentional
- Envisioned
- Not perfect

Blocked
- Discouraged
- Frustrated
- Hurting

FOUR TYPES OF
Christian
Grandparents

Cultural
- Doting
- Supportive
- Playmate

Uninformed
- Unsure
- Unaware
- Unaware of tools

Four Types of Christian Grandparents

Biblical Grandparents are not perfect, but seek to take advantage of every opportunity to influence spiritually. They play hard, love deeply, and sacrifice often for their grandchildren. The biblical grandparent understands that these things are not the end, they are a means to an end so that they can develop a deep relationship with their grandsons and granddaughters that will impact them for eternity.

Cultural Grandparents dearly love their grandchildren and are amazing grandparents by cultural standards, but they have not thought about how they might have a spiritual influence. They have made the means the end, rather than keeping their focus on the greater purpose Scripture reveals.

> To be an intentional Christian grandparent, you must understand your role, work on your relationships, and use your time purposefully.

Blocked Grandparents understand what Scripture says, but they can't act on it because of a barrier such as geographic distance, broken relationships, or divorce. Though some of the greatest heart pains of life come with these barriers, many grandparents are embarrassed to share their pain—they feel alone and don't know what to do. They are in desperate need of the encouragement and support that a grandparenting ministry would bring.

Uninformed Grandparents have never explored the tools created to disciple children and grandchildren. They have not invested the time or resources to be a spiritual influencer to their grandchildren.

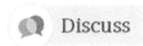 **Discuss**

1. What is your one-phrase response to what you have heard so far?

2. How do you see the lure of leisure promoted in our culture? How has this impacted the way you grandparent?

3. Which of the 4 types of grandparents describes you best— Biblical, Cultural, Blocked, or Uninformed?

4. What books have you read on Christian grandparenting?

5. What is one way you can be more intentional in passing on your faith to your grandchild?

Notes

_____

_____

What the Bible Says About Grandparenting

What the Bible Says About Grandparenting

Two Assumptions

1. _____ is different from _____.

It's a different role—your responsibilities are different now.

- While you are still the parent (noun), you no longer parent (verb), unless invited. Our parenting days are over; accept your role as different now.

- If you have custody of grandkids, you are both a parent and a grandparent.

2. Grandparents are included in the Bible's definition of "_____."

> *This means the extended family as we know it today and includes children, parents, grandparents, and even great grandparents. It's more of a clan or a tribe.*

Larry Fowler | Founder, Legacy Coalition

The Grandparents' Role

1. Grandparents have _____ _____ _____ .
   GENESIS 2:24

We are disciple-making influencers in the lives of our grandchildren. We are another voice to point them to the truth of the gospel.

2. Grandparents have a position of _____ . EXODUS 20:12

- This doesn't end when we leave home.

- This is the first commandment of the Ten Commandments regarding horizontal relationships.

- Grandparents are to be honored, AND it is an honor to be a grandparent.

- Proverbs 17:6 tells us that it is a crowning glory to be a grandparent.

Our parenting days are over – it's time to accept our role as different now!

Larry Fowler | Founder, Legacy Coalition

3. Grandparents have a _____ -_____ responsibility. DEUTERONOMY 4:9

- Messages come at us from many sources that we are not needed and are unimportant. (It isn't just culture; sometimes it is our church or our church leaders.)

- God's Word tells us we have a significant role in our family that continues until the day we go home to be with Jesus.

The 1/2/4/ALL Formula

 Watch One

Only be careful, and watch yourselves closely so that you do not forget the things your eyes have seen or let them slip from your heart as long as you live...

DEUTERONOMY 4:9A

 Teach Two

...Teach them to your children and to their children after them.

DEUTERONOMY 4:9B

 Think Four

He commanded our ancestors to teach their children, so the next generation would know them, even the children yet to be born, and they in turn would tell their children.

 Bless All

The LORD bless you and keep you; the LORD make His face to shine upon you and be gracious to you, the LORD lift up His countenance upon you and give you peace.

NUMBERS 6:24-26

1. Watch One – Yourself

- Don't forget the incredible things God has done for you.

- We should be the most Godly we have ever been during this season of life.

- Make sure the things you have seen God do stay fresh in your mind.

- Don't let your faith or your trust in the Lord slip!

- You can be an incredible influence just by how you live your life.

2. Teach Two – Your children AND your grandchildren

The Biblical ideal is for every child to have six spiritual mentors: two parents and four grandparents.

3. Think Four – Your grandchildren's grandchildren

It is vital that we have a four-generation vision that the two generations not yet born would follow God.

- Picture two generations in the future that are not yet born—that's the vision in this passage.

- We must ponder "What kind of grandparent do I have to be so that my grandchildren will carry on the same faith legacy to their grandchildren?"

4. Bless All - Give and be a blessing to all of these generations

Christian grandparents must regularly evaluate how they are being a blessing to their children and grandchildren. In addition, we may want to pronounce God's favor on them in the Levitical Blessing. We'll discuss this more in Session 5.

The Bible's Job Description for Grandparents

Think of a relay race...

- Think of yourself as runner number _____ .

- Think of the baton as your legacy of _____ .

- Remember the goal of the race is for runner number _____ to finish.

- You must run _____ .

- You must not drop the baton.

- The problem: in a relay race, the runners usually _____ after they pass the baton.

A Better Image...

The passing of an _____ torch.

- You hold it _____ .

- You pass it to the next _____ .

- You run _____ the next runner.

Close your eyes and think about your grandchildren.
Now think about the day when they will be grandparents.
Those little ones yet to be born are part of your legacy!

Discuss

1. Has the passing of faith in your family looked more like the relay race or like the passing of the Olympic torch? Describe your situation.

2. Discuss some ways you struggle with accepting your new role now that your child is the parent and you are the grandparent.

3. How have you felt marginalized or unimportant during this season of life? Does this come from culture, your church, or your family?

4. If you have parents who are still living, how are you placing them in a position of honor? Can you expect your own children to honor you if you are not modeling this well?

5. Share about a time you felt honored by your child or grandchild.

6. What is the goal in passing the Olympic torch? Are you doing that with intentionality? Are you running well? Are you holding your faith high? Are you running beside all the members of your family? Or have you stopped running—as in a relay race?

As you leave this session, make it your goal to finish strong!

Notes

_____

_____

What the Bible Says About Grandparenting

How Do I Teach?

1. Tell _____ _____ :

Tell your children and grandchildren how I dealt harshly with the Egyptians and how I performed my signs among them, and that you may know that I am the LORD. EXODUS 10:2

Don't let your faith stories die out—tell them again and again!

- Tell your grandchildren things you have seen God do.

- Tell them the story of when you trusted Christ as your Savior.

- Tell them stories of how God has worked in your life.

- Tell them how you know the Bible is true and God is real.

- Tell them how God has been faithful through the seasons of life.

- Tell them specific ways you have seen God's provision.

> *The promises of God are not worn out by the passage of time.*

Alistair Begg | Senior Pastor, Cleveland's Parkside Church

2. Establish spiritual family _____ :

The Jews took it upon themselves to establish the custom that they and their descendants and all who join them should without fail observe these two days every year… These days should be remembered and observed in every generation by every family, and in every province and in every city. And these days of Purim should never cease to be celebrated by the Jews, nor should the memory of them die out among their descendants. ESTHER 9:27-28

Traditions are good—traditionalism is not! Many Christians have downplayed traditions out of a desire to avoid traditionalism so much that they have lost teaching opportunities.

Traditions are an important way of passing down our faith. These special celebrations should be a time for our grandchildren to look forward to as they learn about the meaning of special holidays and days that have marked our faith in a significant way.

Commemorate this day, the day you came of Egypt, out of the land of slavery, because the Lord brought you out of it with a mighty hand. EXODUS 13:3

Mark it. Celebrate it. Remember it with a tradition.

3. Influence through our _____ _____ :

Tell it to your children, and let your children tell it to their children, and their children to the next generation. JOEL 1:3

There are four generations in this passage. The first is the teller, then three generations to tell. Here is what you can tell them:

- You are in a privileged position during hard times – a position to be an example of trusting God no matter the circumstances.

- It's the tough times that make the lessons stick.

- In the hardest of times, God can bring victory. He is still in control. He is going before you and with you. You can trust Him. He is always faithful.

Be a perspective giver to your grandchildren so that they will make it through the tough times ahead.

Our days may come to seventy years, or eighty, if our strength endures; yet the best of them are but trouble and sorrow, for they quickly pass, and we fly away. Teach us to number our days, that we may gain a heart of wisdom. PSALM 90:10, 12

4. Identify _____ :

And Joshua set up at Gilgal the twelve stones they had taken out of the Jordan. He said to the Israelites, "In the future when your descendants ask their parents, 'What do these stones mean?' tell them, 'Israel crossed the Jordan on dry ground.'" JOSHUA 4:20-22

A monument can be something you establish or refer back to that helps you remember the Word and works of God in the past.

5. Teach through _____ _____ _____ :

Tie them as symbols on your hands and bind them on your foreheads. Write them on the doorframes of your houses and on your gates. DEUTERONOMY 6:8-9

- Use Christian jewelry (e.g., necklaces, bracelets) that tells your grandchildren you stand for faith, truth and love.

- Be intentional about your home décor (e.g., Levitical Blessing) to impress upon your family the importance of God's Word as part of your legacy.

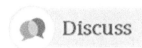 **Discuss**

1. Describe a time that you have seen God work in a powerful way in your life. Have you ever shared this same story with one of your grandchildren?

2. Share about a hard time in your life or the life of your family. What perspective did you gain that you could offer to your grandchildren when they face a difficulty?

3. Consider some new family traditions that have spiritual meaning— maybe a rite of passage for a teen where you take them on a special outing or trip to celebrate this new season of life. Use this time to share your testimony of God's faithfulness, or how you came to a saving faith in Christ.

4. What traditions did your parents or grandparents pass down in your family that made a significant impact on your life? How have you continued to pass these on to your children and grandchildren?

Notes

_____

_____

_____

_____

_____

_____

Reaching the Heart of Your Grandchild

Reaching the Heart of Your Grandchild

Why Target the Heart?

1. Whenever spiritual training is mentioned in the Biblical text, _____ _____ **is not far away.**

The heart is the destination for the Word of God. Your strategy is to impact the hearts of your grandchildren, so that the Word dwells richly in them.

- *Lay hold of my words with all your heart...*
  PROVERBS 4:4

- *These words which I command you today are to be in your hearts.*
  DEUTERONOMY 6:6

- *I have hidden your words in my heart that I might not sin against you.*
  PSALM 119:11

- *Write my words on the tablet of your heart.*
  PROVERBS 7:3

- *My son, do not forget my teaching, but keep my commandments in your heart.*
  PROVERBS 3:1

- *Lay up these words of mine in your heart and in your soul.*
  DEUTERONOMY 11:18

2. My heart is where I _____ .

- *For as he* [a man] *thinks in his heart, so is he…*
  PROVERBS 23:7

- *A good person produces good deeds from a good heart, and an evil person produces evil deeds from an evil heart. Whatever is in your heart determines what you say.*
  LUKE 6:45 (NLT)

Core Essence of Heart

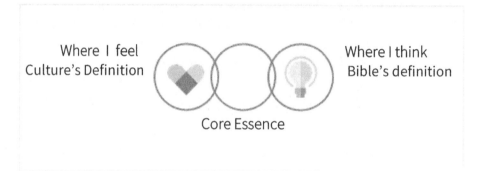

Where I feel
Culture's Definition

Where I think
Bible's definition

Core Essence

3. The Bible's pattern for discipleship:

Finally, brothers, whatever is true, whatever is honorable, whatever is just, whatever is pure, whatever is lovely, whatever is commendable, if there is any excellence, if there is anything worthy of praise, think about these things. What you have learned and received and heard and seen in me — practice these things, and the God of peace will be with you.
PHILIPPIANS 4:8-9

> Our strategy must be to impact the thinking of our grandchildren.

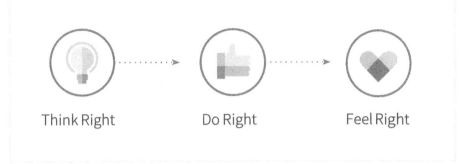

Think Right   Do Right   Feel Right

- God's strategy for discipleship is the opposite of what culture says.

- Culture says, "If it feels right, do it. If it feels bad, then change the way you think."

- God says, "If you think right and do right, you will feel right."

> How our grandchildren think is the most important thing about them. If God can use us to help them think right, we will see that lead to proper actions, which will lead to peace.

 Discuss

1. How can you impact the thinking of your teenage grandchild?

2. How can you impact their thinking when you live far away from your grandchildren?

3. Share a time when you got closer to a grandchild to impact them.

Reaching the Heart of Your Grandchild

Impact like Jesus

1. Like Jesus, we must be _____ .

Jesus was a master of impacting thinking—He aimed at the heart!

Definition of a **purposeful** grandparent:

- Impacts grandchildren through vision and direction
- Has a clear, deeply compelling sense of purpose

Purposeful Grandparents are...	We see this in Jesus	Examples from His ministry
unmoved by lesser issues. They can discern between the very important and lesser issues with both their adult children and their grandchildren.	Cultural or societal barriers did not hinder Him.	He approached the Samaritan woman. (JOHN 4) He healed the invalid beggar. (JOHN 5)
big picture people. They see beyond behavior and actions to principles and outcomes.	He saw issues in light of a much greater picture.	He saw rich people's offerings (and the widow's) differently than others saw them. (LUKE 21:1-4)
reinforcers of critical truths. They revisit and review often the things their grandchildren absolutely must know.	He repeated main truths with the disciples often.	Compare MATTHEW 14:33 with 16:13. When the disciples had just affirmed who He was, He still brought it up again.
challenging with a vision.	He challenged others with significant vision.	He told Peter and Andrew, "I will make you fishers of men." (MARK 1:16-17)

2. Like Jesus, we must be _____ .

Definition of a **passionate** grandparent:

- Impacts grandchildren through a deep and transparent passion
- Is driven by an abiding and deeply-felt emotion

Passionate Grandparents are…	We see this in Jesus	Examples from His ministry
driven by passion. They deeply desire to be used by God to meet the spiritual needs of their grandchildren.	when He saw the multitudes.	When He saw the multitudes, He was moved with compassion. (MATTHEW 9:36-38)
transparent. They are not afraid to let the grandkids see their passion, and they understand the impact of their emotions.	when His emotion was observable to others with Him.	He was visibly angry when the disciples rebuked the parents. (MARK 10:13-15)
appropriate emotion. Their emotion is controlled; not bottled up, but not excessive or improper.	when He grieved for people and grieved over sin.	Jesus grieved over personal loss. (JOHN 11:33-35) He grieved over spiritual hardness. (LUKE 19:41-42)

Misplaced anger can impact hearts for years—separates, isolates, and causes bitterness between family members.

If you understand the power of your passion, it can exert incredible leverage to influence the way your grandchildren think.

Emotion is a highway to the heart!

3. Like Jesus, we must excel in _____ _____ .

Definition of a **personal** grandparent:

- Impacts grandchildren through a personal relationship
- Deeply touches grandkids on an intimate level

Like Jesus, you can leverage this love relationship you have with your grandchild into something that impacts their thinking.

Personal Grandparents are…	We see this in Jesus	Examples from His ministry
alert to heart issues. They look for open doors to deal with spiritual issues in the hearts of their grandchildren.	whenever He engaged people in conversations.	Jesus turned Nicodemus' compliment into an opportunity to address a heart issue. (JOHN 3:1-18)
alert to teachable moments. They leverage a private conversation into an opportunity to teach.	in His unexpected conversations.	He took the opportunity to not only build a relationship, but teach the woman at the well. (JOHN 4)
sensitive to needs. They seek to know the heart needs of their grandchildren and do what they can to meet them.	when He went outside of cultural norms to minister.	He touched a leper! (MARK 1:41)

4. Like Jesus, we must impact the heart through _____.

Definition of a **"perspective"** grandparent:

- Impacts grandchildren through interactive conversations, ideas, and deep thinking
- Molds the thinking processes of grandkids

Perspective Grandparents are...	We see this in Jesus	Examples from His ministry
counterintuitive. Their words are often unexpected in light of today's culture, but they are also true.	when He gave a new perspective of the Law and its application.	Turn the other cheek. (MATTHEW 5:38-39) Whoever humbles himself shall be the greatest... (MATTHEW 18:4)
challenge wrong thinking. They can identify unbiblical assumptions and know how to lovingly confront them.	in His sermons and in His actions.	He challenged sins of the heart. (MATTHEW 5:21-22) He ate with tax collectors and sinners. (MATTHEW 9:11-12)
create learning opportunities. They seek to know the heart needs of their grandchildren and do what they can to meet them.	when He turned everyday events into teaching moments.	He pointed out the fig tree. (MATTHEW 24:32-35)

The challenge is to do this in a way that will be accepted.
We need to confront lovingly!

Personal **Reflection**

1. Which of the four approaches comes easiest to you? (Purposeful, Passionate, Personal, Perspective)

2. Think of your different grandchildren. Is one approach especially needed with one (or more) of them right now?

3. What do you think is the strategy you might need to undertake more intentionally right now?

 ## Discuss

1. What "lesser issues" do you (or other grandparents you know) need to overlook?

2. Share a time when your grandchildren have observed your spiritual passion?

3. How could you leverage relationships to deal with the heart issues of your grandchildren?

4. Describe a time when you have been able to take advantage of a teachable moment with a grandchild?

Notes

_____

_____

Overcoming the
Barriers of Distance

Overcoming the Barriers of Distance

Kinds of Distance

- Most barriers to intentional grandparenting can be summarized by the word _____ .

- These barriers come in three forms:

  1. _____

  2. _____

  3. _____

- The most difficult of these comes when there is both _____

- and _____ distance.

- _____ of us have an adult child who has_____.

  _____   _____   _____ .

- Many grandparents do not talk about this—we may be embarrassed or even feel it is our fault for the way that we parented our children. If this is you... you are not alone! It's a common problem and we want to encourage and help each other through these obstacles.

Responding to Geographical Distance
Three Principles

1. _____ as much as you can.

   - Change your strategy as they grow.

   - Learn to use technology.

   - Don't forget the old methods.

   - Enter their world to communicate best with them.

2. Spend _____ _____ with each one.

   - Get the parents' support.

   - Make it enjoyable to your grandchild.

   - Don't do an "information dump" when you get them alone.

3. Create _____ through special events.

   - Cousin's Camp, or Camp Grammy and Papa.

   - Educational/spiritual/family history excursions.

   - Family reunions.

> *When there is geographical distance, there are some tips I would encourage you to do…be motivated by it; don't use it as an excuse; don't see it as an obstacle that you can't overcome; and stay connected.*

Wayne Rice | Author, Long Distance Grandparenting

Two Reminders of What to Do When There is a Barrier

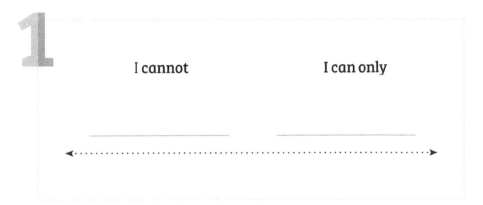

1

I cannot   **I can only**

- Do not live your life in the 'what if' or 'if only' mode.

- No regrets allowed!

- Don't hang on to the past—it's too late to change it!

- You have to deal with the reality as it is now—focus on NOW to move forward into the future.

You can't go back and change the beginning, but you can start where you are and change the ending.

C.S. Lewis

2

_____   _____

_____   _____

_____   _____

_____   _____

_____   _____

I cannot   I can only

_____   _____

- You cannot change others—only they and God can do that!

> When we talk about overcoming obstacles, it's not about getting someone else to change. It is about what we can do different and how we can change ourselves, so we become an agent for God to use as He does the changing of people in our lives.
>
> **Larry Fowler | Founder, Legacy Coalition**

Responding to Relational Distance
The Control/Influence Principle

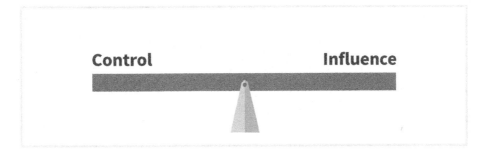

- Parenting is the process of letting go of control.

- Therefore, as a grandparent, you have _____ control.

- The more you attempt to control, the more you
  lose influence.

- Control comes through parental authority.

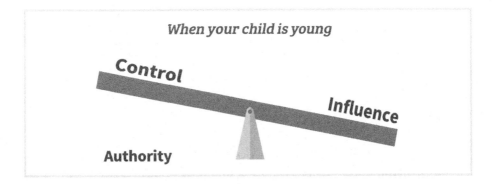

Advice, when unsolicited, is usually received as criticism (and it is really an attempt to control.)

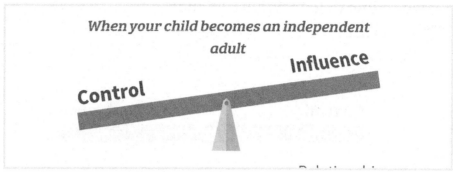

When your child becomes an independent adult

Control

Influence

- Influence comes through a _____ .

Principle:

- The _____ of our influence is directly proportional to the _____ of our relationship.

Start Today...

- Identify what is causing the break and what you can do to repair the relationship.

- Work on repairing or rebuilding relationships—if you don't, you will have no chance to influence for the sake of the gospel.

- Focus on constructive _____ , not destructive _____ .

- Replace control with influence! Good parenting is when you let go with all ten fingers—it's a process, finger by finger.

> It can be easy to revert to "control" when problems begin for our children as adults. Remember, your influence will go down when you try to control their actions and decisions.

Discuss

1. What barrier is the most present for you as a grandparent? Are you hopeless about the situation or have you found ways to overcome it?

2. What are some ways that you stay connected with your grandkids who live a distance from you?

3. What could you do to initiate the re-establishment of the relationship with your adult child?

4. Do you struggle with living in the past? What are some ways that you can let go of the past (good or bad) and move forward into the future? How has this or will this impact your family?

5. Think of a family member that you would like to change or have tried to change. How did that work out for you? Share a lesson you learned from this situation with your group.

6. What are some ways that you have tried to control members in your family? Has this impacted your influence positively or negatively?

Notes

Overcoming the Barriers of Distance

Responding to Spiritual Distance
The Grace/Truth Challenge

Premise:

If our adult children or their spouses have walked away from God, we likely remain the only "Jesus" in their lives.

> And the Word became flesh and dwelt among us, and we have seen His glory, glory as of the only Son from the Father, full of grace and truth.
>
> John 1:14

Jesus was 100% grace AND 100% truth!

When Jesus dealt with people, did He lead with truth or did He lead with grace?

When Jesus dealt with: He led with:

Disciples ⟶   _____

Pharisees ⟶   _____

Sinners ⟶   _____

He led sinners with grace so they would receive truth. Leading sinners with truth, unless the Holy Spirit prepares their hearts, can possibly build walls higher.

Truth statements sound like:	Grace statements sound like:
The Bible says…	Silence
You really should…	I'd like to understand
Your kids need to…	Please forgive me

- If they need to hear the _____ , they may only hear it if you offer _____ first.

- Therefore, we must develop a _____ , so our adult children and their spouses will hear _____ and accept _____ .

- We lead with **grace** so that others will accept **truth**.

- We lead with **truth** so that others will find **grace**.

> *Truth without grace crushes people and ceases to be truth. Grace without truth deceives people and ceases to be grace… The world is weary of all the counterfeit Christs made in the image of grace-despising and truth-despising hearts. People thirst for the real Jesus. Nothing less can satisfy. Grace and truth are His fingerprints. We show people Jesus only when we show them grace and truth. Anything less than both is neither.*

Randy Alcorn | The Grace and Truth Paradox

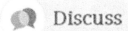 ## Discuss

1. Do you typically lead with your grace foot or your truth foot? Do you find it awkward to lead with grace?

2. In your situation, what needs to lead—grace or truth? Share this with your group.

3. How could you initiate a strategy of leading with grace where it is needed? Make a plan and take a step in that direction this week.

4. How could you initiate a strategy of leading with truth where it is needed? Make a plan and take a step in that direction this week.

Notes

The 8 Best Practices of Christian Grandparents

The 8 Best Practices of Christian Grandparents

This session is based almost entirely on chapter 7 of *Biblical Grandparenting*, authored by Dr. Josh Mulvihill. Listed below are the most common spiritual practices Dr. Mulvihill found in his research on Christian grandparents.

1 Spiritual Practice

Ask Questions

A practice used to generate discussion, create spiritual dialogue, build relationships, and understand what grandchildren believe.

- Become question-asker, rather than advice-giver.

- Ask better questions.

- Use a catechism.

- Be genuinely interested in their interests.

Key Resource

Let's Talk

2 Spiritual Practice

Intentional Meals

An opportunity to discuss matters of faith, teach God's Word to grandchildren, pass on family history, and talk about the events of the day.

- Make it enjoyable for all.

- Pray before you eat—and explain why.

- Put technology away.

- Stay for the conversation.

- Ask purposeful questions: what made you sad, what made you glad, what made you mad today (or in the last week, or month)?

Key Resource

Table conversations

Your grandchildren stand on the shoulders of faithfulness. Faithfulness will solidify your legacy.

Crawford Loritts | Author & Sr. Pastor, Fellowship Bible Church

3 Spiritual Practice

Prayer

The practice of praying with or praying for grandchildren. Common prayers include spiritual protection, physical health, salvation, and daily wisdom as they make life decisions and choices.

- Pray _____ – *The earnest prayer of a righteous person has great power and produces wonderful results.* JAMES 5:16, NLT

- Pray like you mean it!

- Stay focused.

- Be sincere.

- Trust God – He has the power to produce wonderful results.

- Pray _____.

- _____ _____ you are praying for them.

- _____ _____ prayer requests.

Key Resource

Prayer Desk Pad

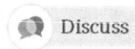 **Discuss**

1. Think about these three areas:
- Asking Questions

- Intentional Meals

- Prayer

2. Share your practical ideas with one another and take notes on some creative ways that you would like to implement them with your grandchildren.

Notes

_____

_____

_____

_____

_____

_____

The 8 Best Practices of Christian Grandparents

4 Spiritual Practice

Teaching

The practice of mentoring grandchildren by passing on wisdom that has been accumulated through a lifetime of experience. Common teaching topics include life lessons, social skills, manners, godly morals, and Biblical truth.

- _____, don't merely _____.

- Teach morals and truth through life skills.

- Use decor of your home as teaching tools. (DEUTERONOMY 6:6-9)

Key Resource

Godly wisdom

We are drowning in information but starving for wisdom.

Alistair Begg | Author & Pastor of Cleveland's Parkside Church

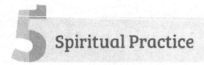

5 Spiritual Practice

Bible Reading & Memory

The practice of reading the Bible with grandchildren, memorizing Scripture together, teaching grandchildren to develop spiritual habits, and giving them their first Bible.

- Have age-appropriate Bible storybooks and Bibles in your home.

- Watch Christian movies with your grandkids.

- Gift them a Bible.

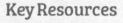

Key Resources

The Bible

Grandkids Promise Cards

_____ my prayer for you is that you will become more like Jesus each day. May you grow and become strong. And may God fill you with wisdom, and grant you favor with all people. Luke 2:40 is my blessing over you.

My precious _____, as I look at your perfectly formed face, I can see the handiwork of God! You are perfectly and wonderfully made. Don't ever believe anything but this wonderful truth! Psalm 139:14 tells how God made you.

6 Spiritual Practice

Telling God Stories

The practice of telling grandchildren the work of God in their life, which includes a grandparent's conversion, God's provision, God's faithfulness, and God's presence in their life.

- Share your testimony with your grandchildren.

- Record them for future generations in writing, audio, or video.

Key Resource

Personal testimony

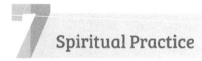

Spiritual Practice

Share the Gospel

The practice of verbally stating the gospel to grandchildren and inviting them to respond in faith.

- Don't leave it up to the church!

- Plan how you will communicate it on their level.

- Make a point of letting them know how important it is.

Key Resource

Gospel message

About 75% of people in America place their faith in Jesus Christ between the ages of 5 and 13. This is the time when they are most likely to accept the gospel message.

Larry Fowler | Founder, Legacy Coalition

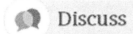 **Discuss**

1. Give ideas and suggestions on these four practical methods:

- Teaching

- Bible reading and Scripture memory

- Telling God-stories

- Sharing the gospel

Make notes of valuable ideas from others in your group.

Notes

_____

_____

_____

_____

_____

_____

The 8 Best Practices of Christian Grandparents

8 Spiritual Practice

Blessing

A practice of pronouncing God's favor upon a grandchild.

- Prayer (intercessory) is communicating to _____ on behalf of _____.

- Blessing is communicating to _____ on behalf of _____ .

- Levitical Blessing:

  The Lord bless you and keep you;
  The Lord make His face shine upon you
  And be gracious to you;
  The Lord lift up His countenance upon
  you And give you peace.

  NUMBERS 6:24-26

The blessing is a powerful tool in the hand of a grandparent to bring God's favor on your grandchild. Who better than the patriarch or matriarch to pronounce God's favor on the family line to follow!

Larry Fowler | Founder, Legacy Coalition

3 Kinds of Blessings

- A Scripture (Levitical or other)
  Reciting Scripture over your grandchild.

- Converting prayer to a blessing
  Instead of addressing the prayer to God on behalf of your grandchild, address the blessing to your grandchild on behalf of God. May the Lord…

- A custom blessing
  Customize your blessing with Scripture or special thoughts about your grandchild.

5 Elements of a Blessing*

- A meaningful touch

- A spoken message

- Attaching high value

- Picturing a special future

- An active commitment

Key Resource
Spoken blessing

From The Blessing by John Trent and Gary Smalley

Group Activity

1. Learn and recite the Levitical Blessing:

   The Lord bless you and keep you;
   The Lord make His face shine upon
   you And be gracious to you;
   The Lord lift up His countenance upon
   you And give you peace.

   NUMBERS 6:24-26

2. Practice giving the Levitical Blessing to someone else in your group (not your spouse).

This Week on Your Own

1. Give the Levitical Blessing to one or more of your grandchildren as soon as you have an opportunity. When you do, include these elements:

   - Use a meaningful touch (hand on head, etc.)

   - Look each other in the eyes

   - Recite the Levitical Blessing as you smile at them

2. Write a custom, spoken blessing for your grandchildren. As you write it, be sure to include the principles from Trent and Smalley's book, The Blessing (see previous page.) Then when you deliver it, make it a special occasion!

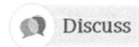 **Discuss**

1. Share your impressions of the eight best practices.

2. What is something you've found to be effective that could be added to the list?

Notes

Becoming an Intentional Christian Grandparent

Becoming an Intentional Christian Grandparent

What is an Intentional Christian Grandparent?

Intentional Christian grandparents build strong

_____ with both the parents and the

grandchildren, and approach every interaction as an opportunity

to

_____ their _____ , and

_____ to future generations.

Work on the relationships you have with your adult children and their spouses. Strong relationships with both parents are essential in order to influence your grandchildren.

> *Don't give up! You are their parent. The potential is still there for a great relationship—and great influence. Never stop reaching out; never stop loving. Remember, God continues to relentlessly pursue people no matter how they respond to Him.*

Larry Fowler | Overcoming Grandparent Barriers

An Intentional Christian Grandparent Goes Beyond...

1. **Spoiling:** One who is focused upon intentionally _____ future generations for good and for God. It's not about indulging!

2. **Failure:** One who uses his/her own _____ (whatever it may be) as a tool of influence. Use it for good! Be transparent.

3. **Hurt:** One who sets aside past hurts by an adult child and offers _____ for the future. Humble yourself. Let it go. Forgive. Move on.

4. **Retirement:** One who develops a _____ to overcome barriers and continues to work at passing on faith to future generations. Take days of rest, not years of rest.

Notes

_____

_____

_____

_____

_____

_____

_____

What's Next for You

Visit legacycoalition.com

- Sign up for monthly newsletter (pop-up screen)
- Register for Grand Monday Nights (legacycoalition.com/grand-monday-nights)
- Leverage resources (legacycoalition.com/store)
- Listen to podcast (legacycoalition.com/podcast)
- Follow our blog (legacycoalition.com/blog)
- Attend the annual Legacy Grandparenting Summit

What's Next for Your Church

- Form a core group
- Get your pastor's support
- Begin to equip grandparents
    - Grandparenting Matters classes/small groups
    - Periodic grandparenting events
    - Be a site host for the Summit

Want to learn more about starting a grandparenting ministry in your church?

Check out Equipping Grandparents: Helping Your Church Reach and Disciple the Next Generation. Written by family ministry experts to encourage church leaders to think about a demographic that has been overlooked and under-resourced in most churches: grandparents.

Available at legacycoalition.com/store

My Declaration

I am a grandparent, and this is my declaration.

Yes, I am a grandparent,
But I am more than a
grandparent, I am a Christian
grandparent.

I believe in the Bible, and the God of the Bible.
I have received the grace of the gospel, of the Christ of the Bible
And I desire to be a life-long devoted disciple.
I want my grandchildren to do the same!

Yes, I am a Christian grandparent. But I am more than that;
I am an intentional Christian grandparent, and this is my declaration.

I love my grandkids,
so I will hold them when they're
born, Cuddle them when they're
one, Chase them when they're two,
Read to them when they're three,
Play with them when they're
four,
And laugh at their jokes when they're five.

I'll support them, exhort them, cheer them, revere them,
I'll praise them, even help raise them —
I will be there for them!
But that's not enough.

As an intentional Christian Grandparent, I will do
more! I will pass on my faith.
No, I will perpetuate my faith.

Therefore, I will teach two generations.
But I will not only teach two generations, I will think four generations.

I will ponder, "What kind of grandparent must I be
So my grandchild becomes one like me — and then his carries on the legacy?"

Yes, I am an intentional Christian grandparent.

Culture says, "Go play."
I say, "No thanks, I'll pray."
Culture says, "Pursue
affluence." I say, "I'll pursue
influence."
Culture says, "You're old — You did your time."
I say, "Not so, I'm in my prime."
Culture says, "Those young people — you can't
relate." I say, "Ain't true — my influence is great!"

I know my grandchildren need me. But from me they need:
Godly wisdom,
My Christ-like example,
My faith stories,
My earnest prayers,
My uninterrupted time,
My unconditional love, and
My God-authorized blessing.

So what is intentional Christian grandparenting? Let me spell it out for you…

I will: **G**uide grandkids with grace
I will: **R**espect parent roles
I will: **A**bound in my affection
And   **N**urture their nature
I will: **D**eal with the dilemma of distance
I will: **P**ray with passion and purpose
I will: **A**djust my attitude, in case I need to
      Restore
relationships I will: **E**xcel
in my example I will:
Number my days
I will: **T**ell them my testimony
I will: **I**ntentionally influence
I will: **N**ever neglect the newest generation. Most
importantly I will: **G**ive them the gospel

I am an intentional Christian grandparent.

name: _____   date: _____

Discover More

Grandparenting Resources

 Free Webinars

Join us for Grand Monday Nights—register on our website, or text 'Grand' to 97000, and watch live, or as a replay. A variety of guests will bring valuable insight and teaching on topics related to how grandparents can practically pass their faith down to future generations.

legacycoalition.com/grand-monday-nights

 Blog

Read our weekly posts for encouragement, expert advice on tricky family dynamics, ideas for things to do with your grandchildren, and more!

legacycoalition.com/blog

 Newsletters

Great way to stay connected for latest updates, news, and teaching from our team at Legacy Coalition. Sign up for this free monthly email.

legacycoalition.com/newsletter

 Podcasts

Legacy Grandparenting can be found on legacycoalition.com or your favorite podcast station. Listen in on engaging interviews with a variety of speakers as they talk about navigating today's world as a Christian grandparent.

legacycoalition.com/podcast

 Seminars

Learn what the Bible says about your role as an intentional Christian grandparent. Host or attend Grandparenting Matters at your church or small group. This six-session series will encourage, inspire, and equip grandparents, and is available in three formats to fit your needs.

legacycoalition.com/seminars

 Conferences

Gather with other Christian grandparents for the annual Legacy Summit at a city near you. This conference features some of the top national speakers who will bring inspiration, encouragement, and ideas to help you build a lasting spiritual legacy in your family.

legacycoalition.com/summit

Access all Legacy Coalition resources at LegacyCoalition.com

Grandparenting Matters
Book Series

Biblical Grandparenting
Dr. Josh Mulvihill

Biblical Grandparenting explains culture's misleading messages about grandparenting, provides a biblical overview of the role of grandparents, and shares groundbreaking research that will give grandparents, students, pastors, and future leaders a vision to impact the next generation for Christ.

Overcoming Grandparenting Barriers
Larry Fowler

Overcoming Grandparenting Barriers is a helpful guide to influencing your grandchildren's lives even through discouraging or hurtful situations in your family. In this book, you will find wisdom, helpful tips, and encouragement to persevere. You will also be reminded that you are not alone in this challenging position.

Discipling Your Grandchildren
Dr. Josh Mulvihill

With an assortment of actionable ideas—from practical tips on how to better connect with your grandchildren to fun, age-appropriate activities— *Discipling Your Grandchildren* is an invaluable tool chest for grandparents who want to build a biblical foundation, lead by example, and point their grandchildren to Christ.

Grand Parenting
Dr. Josh Mulvihill

Grand Parenting gives you a biblical foundation for investing spiritually in your grandchildren and walks you through principles of influencing them for Christ— from sharing the Gospel with unbelieving grandchildren to discipling them to a mature faith in Jesus. God designed you to pass on a rich heritage of faith in Christ.

Raising Your Grandchildren
Cavin Harper

No one expects to be a grandparent raising a grandchild, and it can be a daunting task. But take courage—it can also be a blessing. Let this book be your guide to finding hope and joy in the journey. In *Raising Your Grandchildren*, you'll discover practical tools as well as the encouragement you need to find hope in Christ and strength for the journey ahead.

Long-Distance Grandparenting
Wayne Rice

Many grandparents find themselves geographically separated from their grandchildren. Discover how to turn this obstacle into an opportunity. This book brings practical tools and encouragement to connect with your grandchildren so that you can share God's love and invest in their faith like never before.

Notes

Notes

Notes

Made in the USA
Las Vegas, NV
28 January 2024

84970328R10057